Small Planes
and the
Dead Fathers of Lovers

Candace de Taeye

Guelph, Ontario

Written by Candace de Taeye
© 2016 All rights reserved

Cover image by Holly Crain
© 2016 All rights reserved

ISBN: (pbk) 978-1-928171-42-3
ISBN: (ebk) 978-1-928171-43-0

Vocamus Press
130 Dublin Street North
Guelph, Ontario
N1H 4N4

www.vocamus.net

for

Steve and Rudy, Ty and Tye
and a house named Magnolia Place.

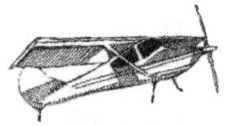

ACKNOWLEDGMENTS

Firstly, a great many thanks to Jeremy Luke Hill for offering to publish these poems, with all the attendant work and negotiating that that entails, and also for graciously welcoming me into the Guelph writing community with many cups of coffee, great conversations at that harvest table, and invitations to literary events around town.

Secondly, an equal amount of thanks to Holly Crain, who drew and painted the cover art, which will be the reason a lot of people pick up this book up off a vendor's table or shelf

Next, I owe a significant amount of what I know about writing poetry to Margaret Christakos. Thanks as well to Jenny Sampirisi, Jay MillAr, Ken Babstock, and Karen Solie, who were also excellent teachers. And to my classmates with their valuable insight and feedback – Zvi Gilbert, Dick Capling, John Bell, Jennifer Lovegrove to name a few. Guelph poets for their input and support – Madhur Anand, Mike Chaulk, Zane Koss, and Adrien Willem.

Thanks also to these folks who have nothing to do with poetry but deserve some thanks for the development of me and of these poems – George and his little yellow Cessna, all of the other pilots, and guides and travel companions, Sebastian Murdoch for selling our 165 year old house, Fred Novotny for books and carving knives, and to Harry Clark and Jack and Alice Burgess for being quality auxiliary grandparents over the years. To my other mother Tracey, my mother-in-law Jacqui, and my nearly mother-in-law Wendy and her son Ty,
To my Mom and Dad,
To my husband Steve
and our son Roe.

Thank you for all the fodder and stories, and words.

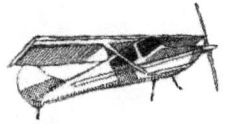

SMALL PLANES AND THE DEAD FATHERS OF LOVERS

Yellow Cessna

first this old man dapper despite his body
odor, worn mink cap. offered me a flight

small yellow Cessna. we flew over the fields tobacco potato
tombstones of dead pets my childhood home a quarry

the whole town could tessellate into
unbeknownst to me. we start and end low

over the house where my future
father-in-law will die in my arms.

decades ago the man in the mink cap was paid
$50 a piece for each snowy owl he trapped.

Farm hands

July's tar is hot sap, syrup that absorbs readily at the wrist once spelling irksome in my head for days. furrow

hand mapping the concentrations of hornworms
in the fields. I was likely then my most genuine self.

it took years and a curry lamb stew recipe to realize Harry, a coworker, another adopted grandfather was illiterate.

snapping the flowers off, they call it topping. here we grow in-dependence, cultivate work ethic, nicotine calm.

Alice, the farm and many neighbours, prominently display the framed aerial photographs of their rural acrerage.

Alice

the isolation of finches made famous the tiny islands
evolving independently on the dead ends of rural roads

she was kind, his second choice, but 60 years later he learned to cook for her. I borrowed eggs, power-tools, sugar and grandparents.

she once scolded me, my dirt bike scaring off migratory birds and a lost racing pigeon. I crafted a wreath of limp songbirds out of spite.

gravestones spring up, granite volcanoes, ashes buried. hers spitting distance, in direct line from the first choice and the pilot son-in-law.

maps discretely embroidered into bomber jacket linings. in this case his ashes. that summer we smoked his humidor clean.

Opportunists

the pigeon who through perseverance became a flower.
I'm still a pigeon, just a pigeon who eats artisanal bread and cheese.

as a child I laid in a snowy field long enough for the vultures to circle.
see how low they'd come. I never even thought of taking a picture.

I didn't know we were poor until the German teacher denied my application for an exchange program. "Who would want to stay here?"

put the fledglings back where you found them. resist the urge
to help. was I different then? before I had ever flown or left?

the arborist seems to think so. I've always called myself
an opportunist. I define poverty in terms of food.

Green Screen

the passage of time layered semi transparent. every boy I've ever kissed here at some point along the trail. land marking epochs.

unspooled familiar static pulling my foot beats along a magnetic cassette ribbon retraced near daily for two dogs or 20 years.

occasionally I'm still present here but most days it's faded some would argue the forest is always a background.

the macro setting the most used feature on my first camera framing the light of under-looked spiders and mushrooms.

I file away a cache of maps, sand, ashes and tiny rocks of significance from this forest and all the tiny islands to come.

Toronto Island

just days after father's day helicopter rotors julienned
the potatoes in the field and the actor's father.

we've married other people, but a photo still sits on his mom's dresser. young actor and I, on an early date. he wore his dad's shark tooth.

a purple bruise. evidence of paintball in the woods the day before.
in one drawer an intricate puzzle box holds the ring he gave me.

I gave it to her when I left town. no more backburner simmer.
while moving a picture of him singing 'little bones' surfaced.

I return to this island often, for the sick carried from the north
inside pipers and cessenas. for the night skyline from the tarmac.

Prince Edward Island

too many tiny mushrooms and the flowers grew out of the wallpaper
until I could remember how to speak again with the one present

I've never travelled far enough, or perhaps just not
long enough, to not find an English speaker.

he was platonic at present and past, but I could imagine an alternate
future. shuffling along the silica sand beach's humming indifference.

"*he's not him only you but better*" few benefits from pairing
up with someone who feels like I do. our dogs/both women

of similar dominance fighting under the surface. people sense
a threat. the roughness of the little shark washed ashore.

Newfoundland

visiting another mother our skirts anchored by skipping
stones watching wary lambs graze under big bad wolf winds.

howling negates conversation, we blow bubbles instead. Allegro gusts
steal these too. pilots them away, pearlescent lemmings

at break neck speed. the next morning collecting wild blueberries
and the bleached bones of small mammals on the tult.

two small boats of tourists, one aiming telescopic lenses, ours donning wetsuits. I fell back off the side to swim with the humpback.

we rarely talk now, since I sold Magnolia Place. left the town
and our histories within it. closing off the house to both of us.

Koh tao

the year New Year's fell on Valentine's, lit strings of firecrackers on the bow. being struck by the paper casings I jumped off.

breathing under the waves long enough for the new ink to leech out of the tattoo the monk claimed represented "betterment of self"

I chose here instead of Haiti. I could have helped with water purification, mobile hospitals. claiming "flights were already booked".

I mixed unlabeled whiskey into the apothecary bottle Redbull, shot big guns, jumped flaming rope, rode motorcycles with no helmet.

watched and gambled on Muay Thai from front row seats. I'll admit to a tiger selfie and taking a lot of photos of the poor.

Iceland

where continents move away from each other, opening up. I bought
next winter's wool socks. worn through shuffling on pine plank floors.

my cousin took a picture of the compass being tapped into my skin.
we talk over a box of wine under the midnight sun and ptarmigans.

the iron particles remain aligned to north on the tops of their beaks'
magnetoreception. the pigeons, their unsightly disposable freedom.

ashes instead of clouds obscure the volcano. we saw all
of ring road. passed on eating the medium rare minke whale.

adulthood becomes about greying, neutrality. my mother becomes
less the hero. my own father starts showing up in more photos.

Cortes

the first time, the actor had dropped off a letter folded over a $50 bill
'for gas'. on the tails side a snowy owl. The road trip's turning point.

all that money never changed him, only seemed to burden him.
the second time, under a honeymoon the arborist and I eloped

and learned to surf. no longer individuals, the sand-saturated waves
had filed off our fingerprints. later realizing my eyes>my stomach

repenting extra oysters back to the ocean. our apologies while tossing
lucky remainders underhanded meters. on the other side of the world

on another island, the actor lived surfing better, under breath
under breath, we can't see up. ankle tether drags us ashore.

Okunoshima

I'm here for the several thousand feral rabbits, congregating around the ruins of a 1970's American style resort and poison gas factory.

with the arborist at home, opening one little letter a day. there was no one to get a picture of me, but there were very photogenic spiders.

conspicuous here, but not quite so as much as the American on the train departing Hiroshima wearing a US Navy sweatshirt.

on an island nearby, a triennial art festival, old fishing village houses gutted now cocooning art installations. saturated with galleries.

Naoshima Insight Guide. the book's only English it's title. I appreciated how little I knew here, my lack of understanding, and bought it.

Sao Miguel

to eat a bowl of stewed finches. tiny bones to make your gums bleed.
he went to see where the girl with the twig owl magnet originated.

their relationship became a dead horse, still warm and comforting
for seasons. genuine erodes when you don't struggle.

not to say they didn't. in 2001, Air Transat flight 236, landed in the
Azores. gliding without fuel longer than any passenger jet in history.

a hurricane grounded our little plane. stranding the arborist, our son
and I. waiting it out eating queijo fresco and punched potatoes.

years ago he asked if I still loved the actor? I always would
in a way there was no longing. since you can't follow all the forks.

Hometown

"for 100 years we had no marker" a felt tip pen is a marker
so is a paintball gun. an indication, indicator, arrow, compass point.

One neighbour, the English teacher who said whatever it was I wrote
wasn't poetry. she was enamored with the actor then drama student.

the other alcoholic neigbour H------! became an island
the day his fiancé jumped out of his speeding car.

the feed store's back wall is an aviary of canaries and finches, then
another cage for unwanted, but undrowned tiger striped barn kittens.

every two weeks I pick up dog food and exchange books with the
owner. his Haitian wife's sequined rum bottle collection upstairs.

Constructions

an assortment of small planes have flown me between
archipelagos and over Rockies, Himalayas and Andes

Peru has 400 varieties of potatoes and dozens of types of corn.
we watch our trail guide stop and photograph the small blooms.

he is compiling an Andean Orchid Guide Book.
classified as a flower a bee would want to copulate with.

he refers to the Incan villages not as ruins
but as constructions. English his third language.

15 years after the crash, I meet the pilot here. he comes to our table
asks if we would mind he and his buddies smoking stogies nearby.

Highway 24

on that first flight I had borrowed my mom's old Nikon camera. She stopped taking pictures after the grey owl landed in our maple tree.

I was born with no sense of direction. The same year David Bowie starred in *Labyrinth*. the intro, an early CGI barn owl, then a lost girl.

The sky was grey, neutral, while attending my parents' last court date. listening to both sides in the same room. how little confidence.

watching a red and white plane crash into the dust that was a field while driving the route between my mother and father's hometowns.

not far from the summer dormant sand and salt storage mountains where my sibling and I would shuffle into the other parent's car.

Float plane

After he died she sold the house by the municipal airport. she moved
to the forest, a reflective lake frontage. sublimates her grief into

a cottage mahal of Canadian shield splendor.
the kitchen island a granite sarcophagus with a fruit bowl.

currently bordered by an assortment of highchairs.
the grandchildren leaving sticky fingerprints on the polished tomb.

following the funeral's low laps of white pigeons, assigned doves
we drove up there to sail the wreaths of flowers off the dock.

the cottage was only a skeleton then. last father's day we spread brie
over baguettes. watched a yellow float plane land across the lake.

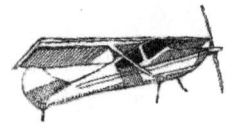

BLUE COLLAR, RED HOOD

rubber smelling mother
I tote your midnight

brown bag to
cross town industries

"how better to see you with my dear"
– in turn –

you drive my lunch
through the woods

(past Dingo
tobacco farm dog)

we share sandwiches
blue collar wishes

ensure my
menial manual labor

oxen work ethic
is cultivated

motivate education
further vicarious living

invaluable wage
unpaid noon hours spent

mother no wolves
not mama wolf

not even a puppy
not that I wanted

one
litter of four

well two by two
sister's half blood

two half sisters
milk teeth meat teeth

liberal mother
not in absentia

shifts factories
single factors

uprooted to country
anti-aseptic better

armed pubescent with
pocket knives crossbow

motorbike mud track
to grandma's door

```
                coyote    coyote
     coyote                              coyote
                  pine
             fell    I    asleep
                forest floor
```

walked home slowly
under yellow eyes

now they are always
watching my back

blind grandfather
unaware the walk home

a race I've just won
sitting on a school bench

waiting

along seven months
burgeoning belly bulge

full of glowing content
– wake up –

grab at a flat
middle sadness

relief new hormones
long for a bump

of bones and skin inside me
not made of chicken meat

at seven I once roosted on
two farm fresh eggs

towel nest a few hours
later confiscated

scrambled eaten

a misunderstanding
the lumberjack

re: Arborist
killed the wolf

it had cancer really
axe euthanasia

inseparable friends
she consoled him

wore the pelt
wore it for him

made love
amidst the wolf blood

she's a mother now
two canine shadows

pad softly along
mud trails

to grandma's
across the forest

….down the muddy hill….over the beaver dam….past the oak…
through the cedar thicket….around the pasture….over the creek…
to mom's house…

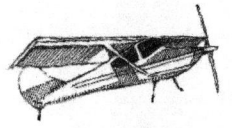

I, HOUSE

home is where the

no,
home is the
heart,
within it we are reoxygenated
recirculated to distant capillaries
(Tofino, Reykjavik, Bangkok) spent
and return exhausted

it outlives us
we die curled up within it

if we are lucky enough

perfusion

circadian propulsion through furnished ventricles

front door aorta

amortization

amortization married, not least.
you my ~~homeowner~~ youngest wife

                                        indebted Atlas

                                        yet single

I- shelter, yours, nameless

a separation

by my last wife
introduced

and her husband

divorcing
smoking menthol cigarettes in the garden

private

        sale

later you'll kill her roses

matte chips

hawthorn yellow

rosemary sprig

concord ivy

samples of these
the former saved
along with delphinium and amaranth seeds-

blew east, settled, married a new house
sowed our colours all over
its walls

vestiges

and before her here
sisters, spinsters
occupied my insides
for sixty years

their traces closeted
thinly veiled
layers of wallpapers

tree rings – between this same
brick, plaster and lathe

intention

my silence intimidated
on our honeymoon
so you high school sweetheart invited
to share the unframed mattress

pick up where you had left
off was the plan
was the impetus for returning hometown

layers

by now interior patina all over
I grow onion layers of others colours

I don't mind sharing
flesh pleasure I lack
sixteen decades
of overwhelming
maturity for anyone

enclose temporary endeavors here

tie limb knots with the soft
spoken french-boy on my shingles

later carve a maritime fiddler belt
notch in the kitchen

convections

frosty clouds exhaled
over cereal

you occluded the vent (ricle)
bent in the cellar furnace-man (tells the spiders)
suction and failed-circulation
my hot breath ceased
silly girl

eighth grade submission
two pages for convections example
using domiciled air exchange

your stepfather's eyes had lit up explaining

why

hot air was below windows

a wedding

maimed birds carried over the threshold
concussed brides in the maw of the cat through the dog's door.

the key

                legal size
                envelope
                multi-digit
                cheque
                triplicate
                copies
                fine print
                forty seven
                signatures

a yellowed slightly torn property survey printed the year you were born

              in the
              bottom
              corner
              of the
              envelope
              a ring shaped
              instead
              as a key
              to carry always

fishing

                                I love you house,

                    but the town, a B. speck, a map mole
                         on southern Ontario's spine
                       circulates too little new blood

                       this suburban luring proves tedious

                                                    lonely

lonely

Germans must have been, here, at the P.O.W camp
      at the edge of town an elephant

sampling the magnolia out front
      on her chaperoned walk from the zoo

long after the boys from the separate school
      replaced the Germans

the Estonian psychologist widower retired
      from the same school, packing up his library

lastly the cantonese business students came
      two of whom beheaded their dean with an axe

specimens

in the basement
a species monopoly
of spiders are kept
well, not often killed

tending dragnets
strung from undersides
of the pine plank floor

they collect and
catalogue my records
of sloughed years

a dining room

supposed to have been
seats books instead
hundreds are kept
for company

                                      as documentation of the unmonumnetal
                                            shaping of one's thoughts

bound presents amongst shelves

        twenty-three minute volumes of Beatrix Potter
        from two decades of bedtimes ago

        a *Joy of Cooking* inherited
        from a grandmother I can't remember

        small books from past lovers with secrets inside

        a tome of Russian fairy tales, a thank you
        for helping an elderly neighbor pack up his life
        to go home
                        to Estonia
                                to die

proprioception:

from Latin *proprius*
meaning "one's own" "individual" and perception
is the sense of the relative position of neighboring parts of the body
relating to stimuli produced and perceived within an organism

exoskeleton

steadily
becoming your body

not just a heart
this space an extension
of your experience

nourish and entertain yourself
inside me
beloved parasite

I can insulate a nude/unkempt/sickly you

as I breath with seasons
floors and window panes adjusting

curb appeal

        matronly figure
        fifties Magnolia
     eclipsing my exterior
         curb appeal

         she was bait

      for the Arborist
timidly coaxed from the city

character

claw-footed slowcooker
door jamb parallelograms
trim-lines blurred with leaden hue
a dozen times over

charms appreciate
don't threaten
to gut and taupe
me

a sweater

a coffee mug

a second toothbrush

then a moving truck shoehorns it in storage solutions upended
re-justified geometry of picture frames moving easels for acoustics
new aesthetics

you knew it was stupid
                       to cry over lost
                                        bookshelf real estate

you ought to share more than the bed

the Arborist

your nest lies in the crook of his branch
exactly one third over the median of the bed

he was years late getting home
insisting on beating a dead horse

refrain

>me here
he wanted this
I wanted him
and here

>and us in this
and ours

>I hesitated
was hurt
was hard for me
to be less of you,
House

FOR SALE – AN ADDENDUM

to mark it

now I have a lure
you've never noticed the hesitant fibers
on magnolia seeds

trawling so near
For Sale

honey

which food never spoils ?   honey
stained floors
      precariously housed in backyard past tents
refinished   for his first birthday

refresh paint
tears tearing up
his nursery considered for a second
bathroom.

salmon tangent

no one is watching you
tossing ghost dimes
to the koi/carp/no salmon
against the current
                          dragons

       change into golden   rolls
                                     demons drunk
                                     neighbor – H-------!
                                   increases the height of the

                                   falls often slur dam(n) the potential
                                   buyers wishing phrased right of way

100 years takes over 3 months

most fish are retracing a
couple straying up/changing shape/getting desperate
falling a part a little maki at the local sushi place one last time

storage unit

he's
encoding
preverbal memories
here's
the street you
named him after

revolve to return
each September
for the same picture

retrieval

half of you is lost
in storage by now

the last open house

I assume the Estonian neighbour died there by

now less frequent conversations with previous owner/other mother

never forget the elephant died full of cancer and french fries

the P.O.W camp is overgrown with weeds, each vertical surface mural

earmarked for demolition a subdivision reincarnation a weekend

destination in good light for photographers and us, displaced

by an open house

just strangers considering layouts

hepatic

maybe not so much a heart
as liver? I'll filter accumulation
of your excess habits imbibing
fatty secrets and night caps

the right force can lacerate you
I'll hemorrhage financially a memorable
expense to help clot the year
foie gras on French toast in the midst of it

tandem

House I love you still sills known
intimately finger these plaster cracks
your creaks in my leg's muscle memory
but this town has grown only from bedrooms

now we're cheating it's not even bridging
keeping sun in empty rooms

yellow chairs

the new interior left entirely 'detachment
grey' you hastily re-sow concord ivy in the kitchen
creamsicle,
parakeet, and
new penny elsewhere

the Arborist assembles an invitation to community
                the oak harvest table

the chairs molded mod polypropylene

            4 white

            2 yellow   these are the chairs that poetry bought

Locard's exchange principle

"every contact leaves a physical trace"
      realtor cards and shoe prints accumulate and
        how long will it take for your vestiges to fade?

"at the same time they will take something away with them"

      same spiders immigrate out from the basement boxes
      you consider mailing a copy of the 'spinster's' deed to the new

titleholder she's twenty something single female professional

hiraeth:

(noun) "a homesickness for a home that you can never return to or that never was"

you ask if the magnolia has started to bloom yet this year?

the year of Sebastians

new at work his partner
refers to him as 'Seb'
a couple of moms
from Lemaze frequently
call their son – 'Bash'

but mainly our realtor's
name on the sign

he's sharp
pants and eager
unnatural salesman
still there's sincerity

our grandfathers play
into this more than he
and I ever let on

refrain

                    me here
                he wanted this
                 I wanted him
                    and here

                and us in this
                    and ours

                  I hesitated
                   was hurt
              was hard for me
              to be less of you
                     House

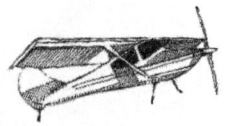

ABOUT THE AUTHOR

Candace de Taeye's poetry has been published in *CV2*, *Carousel*, *Echolocation*, *Feathertale.com* and *Joypuke*. Her first chapbook *Roe* was published by Publication Studio Guelph.

For the last nine years she has worked during the day, and more frequently at night as a paramedic in downtown Toronto. She lives in Guelph with her husband, young son, two dogs, two cats, four elderly tree-frogs and a very large tortoise.

www.ingramcontent.com/pod-product-compliance
Lightning Source LLC
Chambersburg PA
CBHW032211040426
42449CB00005B/540